Negotiation 101

The Absolute Beginner's 20-Minute Guide to the Art of Negotiating: Acquire Basic Negotiator Skills

Table of Contents

Introduction

If you're at a point in your personal or professional life where negotiations are crucial, it can often feel overwhelming. The high-stakes atmosphere can sometimes resemble a battlefield, with each party fighting to come out on top. But what if there's another way? A path that views negotiation as an amicable exchange of ideas and interests, rather than a clash of wills. If this approach appeals to you, then this guide is for you - offering insights into the art of negotiation.

Negotiation isn't just about winning an argument or securing the best deal. It's a delicate balance of communication, empathy, strategy, and psychology. It involves understanding your own needs as well as the needs of the other party. But how does one evolve from a beginner negotiator to a skilled diplomat? This guide aims to illuminate that journey.

Imagine entering a negotiation filled with self-assurance, equipped with a well-thought-out plan. Picture transforming potentially confrontational situations into cooperative dialogues. Consider guiding negotiations in your favor without harming relationships with your counterparts. This isn't an impossible dream, but a reality that can be achieved with the appropriate knowledge and skills.

In this guide, we will talk about the following:

- What is Negotiation?
- Stages of Negotiation
- Situations Where Negotiation is Crucial
- Steps to Master the Art of Negotiation
- Common Negotiation Pitfalls and How to Avoid Them

So, are you prepared to embark on this transformative journey? In the upcoming sections, we will dissect the science and art of negotiation. We'll delve into the psychological foundations of effective negotiation, explore proven strategies, and provide practical tips to elevate your negotiation prowess. Whether you're negotiating a business deal, resolving disputes, or navigating everyday negotiations, this guide is designed to equip you with the necessary tools and knowledge.

Let's shift our mindset from viewing negotiation as an adversarial encounter to a collaborative approach. Let's learn to navigate the intricate dance of diplomacy. Embark on this thrilling journey with the aid of this all-encompassing guide.

Chapter 1: What is Negotiation?

Negotiation is a process wherein people settle differences. It is a form of a give-and-take discussion or conference in an attempt to reach an agreement or settle a dispute. It is a way of discussing issues and arriving at a conclusion that will, as much as possible, benefit all parties. It is a careful exploration of the positions of both parties, with the goal of identifying a decision or course of action that's mutually acceptable, giving both of them their desired demands.

When parties negotiate, they usually expect to give and receive something. While it is true that they have interlocking goals that they cannot accomplish independently, they do not usually want or need the same thing. As such, the output of negotiation can be a win-win or a win-lose situation.

One party will either attempt to force the other party to comply with their demands, modify the adverse position, and move towards compromise, or determine and propose a solution that will meet the objectives of both parties. The nature of the independence between these parties will have a major impact on the nature of their present and future relationships.

Negotiation involves mutual adjustment or the situation where one party will eventually agree to the proposal of the other party, or both parties will adjust depending on their agreed stance. It is true that both parties know that they can influence the outcomes of the agreement in their favor. Negotiation seeks to understand how individuals change their positions throughout the decision-making process, based on the goals that each party seeks to achieve.

As negotiations proceed, one party proposes offers and even counter-offers to changes proposed by another. One party considers the consequences of one action with another, and when it has finally decided, it will change its own proposals. This process of give-and-take and adjust-readjust continues until both parties finally agree to one and only one course of action.

For instance, a person wants to buy a house and lot. He does not hastily go to the company, give his money, and have its title registered under his name. He must undergo negotiation with the agent of the company to make additional inquiries as to the house and lot, mode of payment, specifications, and many more. Only after he finds the answers to these inquiries can he decide whether or not to pursue buying the house.

Another instance is when a person borrows money. The debtor, or the one who borrowed, pays the creditor, or the one who lent, but the latter may impose certain conditions as to its payment, and these conditions are agreed upon by negotiation. For instance, the creditor will let the debtor borrow his money, only if the latter is willing to pay it in installments every month (with interest). If the debtor agrees, the deal is sealed, otherwise, the creditor may offer alternatives, or he may just reject the request of the debtor.

An interesting instance of negotiation is when police officers are in a hostage-taking scene, as seen in movies. The officers, using a megaphone, ask the hostage-takers to bring down their weapons, let the hostages go, and surrender so that they can talk about the issue peacefully and without causing too much harm. A related situation is when a person is captured and his release is conditioned under the payment of a large sum of money. Clearly, negotiation works not only as a problem solver, but also as a link – a bridge that connects the thoughts of two or more people in order to determine or obtain a satisfactory, beneficial, and favorable solution not just for one party, but for all.

Negotiation may come in different terms, depending on where it is used. For instance, negotiation under the law may also involve mediation, mini-trial, arbitration, or early evaluation. In business, negotiation is also known as conflict management and conflict avoidance. In daily life, negotiation is also known as amicable settlement, while in banks it is usually called credit management. No matter what negotiation is called in different fields, they basically work in the same way.

There is no qualification as to who can negotiate. It'd even be safe to say that everyone can negotiate. Anyone can analyze problems like a manager; anyone can efficiently argue like a lawyer; anyone can solve problems like a father; anyone can communicate like an agent. Simply put, anyone can do what a legitimate negotiator does. However, only a few become effective negotiators because it requires knowledge and the mastery of certain skills. Before someone can negotiate, it is necessary for him to know how it works.

Understanding the Basics of Negotiation

Negotiation is an art that requires understanding human nature, communication skills, and strategic thought. It's about finding solutions that satisfy all parties involved. Let's explore win-win negotiation, different styles, and key principles that guide effective negotiation.

The Concept of Win-Win Negotiation

A win-win negotiation is a situation where all parties feel they've achieved something positive. It's an approach where you aim to satisfy not just your own needs, but also those of the other party. This approach fosters mutual respect and collaboration, leading to sustainable agreements and stronger relationships. It's not about getting the largest slice of the pie, but about making the pie bigger so that everyone gets a satisfying piece.

Different Styles of Negotiation

There are various negotiation styles, each with its own strengths and weaknesses. The five main styles include competing, accommodating, avoiding, compromising, and collaborating.

- Competing negotiators assertively pursue their own needs at the expense of others.
- Accommodating negotiators are more cooperative and tend to put the needs of others before their own.
- Avoiding negotiators try to evade the issue instead of confronting it directly.
- Compromising negotiators seek a quick, mutually acceptable solution that partially satisfies both parties.
- Collaborating negotiators seek a win-win solution that fully satisfies all parties involved.

Understanding these styles can help you adapt your approach based on the situation and the people you are negotiating with.

Chapter 2: Stages of Negotiation

Negotiation is not plain talk with the other party. It is not a situation where both parties can just throw every word that they can to get what each wants. As a process, it follows a structured approach in order to achieve a desirable, orderly outcome.

The negotiation process includes the following stages:

Preparation

Preparation is the most important part of the negotiation process. The upcoming discussions must not be based on emotions or purely conjecture so as not to affect the mood of both parties and lead the negotiation to nothingness. As such, before going into it, both parties must be prepared physically, mentally, and emotionally.

Preparation involves the discussion of the following matters:

- **Time and Place:** The parties must be able to decide on the place where the negotiation will be carried out. This is to avoid confusion and further altercation once the day of the meeting arrives. They must also decide on the time when the process will happen.
- **Attendants:** The parties must be able to decide on the people who will and who can attend. This is to avoid unnecessary commentaries and interpolations and to ensure that all people who attend the negotiation will only be parties-in-interest, or those who are directly affected by the outcome of the negotiation.
- **Facts:** The parties must discuss the relevant facts of the case or scenario. This is to ensure that everyone in

the meeting is aware of the situation being talked about, the circumstances surrounding it, and the possible consequences that might arise for every proposed course of action.

- **Arguments:** The parties must be prepared with their arguments. These statements must be based on facts, research, and analysis, and not purely on emotional bursts and conjectures. This is to ensure that all the arguments raised will be fact-based and not merely hearsay.
- **Representatives:** The parties must decide on who their representatives will be. This is to ensure an orderly negotiation process such that only one or more people will talk and raise arguments. This is also to ensure a clear understanding of what a party means to say.
- **Aggrieved Persons:** The parties must be able to determine the aggrieved persons or those who are affected by the situation. For instance, in termination of employment disputes without just cause, the aggrieved persons will be the employees removed from work without just cause. This is to ensure that after the negotiation, a proper course of action or resolution will be made.

Discussion

The discussion stage of negotiation is an essential phase in which members of each party come together to converse about the matter at hand. This stage serves as the foundation for the entire negotiation process, setting the tone for the dialogue that will follow.

One of the primary goals of the discussion stage is to lay out the facts of the situation. Each party presents their understanding of the circumstances, providing a clear picture from their viewpoint. This is crucial as it ensures that everyone involved is on the same page about the context and specifics of the issue being negotiated. This step can help to eliminate any misunderstandings or misconceptions that might exist about the problem.

In addition, the discussion stage also involves identifying both the problem and the aggrieved persons. By explicitly stating the problem, the parties can ensure they are all working towards a common goal. Identifying the aggrieved parties helps to establish who has been affected by the problem and therefore has a stake in the outcome of the negotiation.

Another critical aspect of the discussion stage is dealing with inconsistencies in the sets of facts presented by each party. Discrepancies can often arise due to differing perspectives or interpretations of events. It's not uncommon for each party to have their unique set of facts, shaped by their experiences and viewpoints. These different versions of events can lead to conflict, as each set of facts is designed to protect the interests of the party presenting them.

This is where the challenge lies in the discussion stage. If these differences are not adequately addressed and reconciled, the negotiation may fail. The parties must work hard to find common ground, acknowledging the validity of each other's experiences and working towards a shared understanding of events. This requires open-mindedness, empathy, and a willingness to see things from the other party's perspective.

The discussion stage, therefore, is not just about stating facts and identifying problems and aggrieved parties. It is also about managing differences, reconciling conflicting viewpoints, and building a shared understanding. This stage sets the groundwork for the rest of the negotiation process, making it an integral part of any successful negotiation.

Clarification

The clarification stage is a vital part of the negotiation process that follows the initial discussion. This phase acts as a bridge between understanding each party's viewpoint and finding a middle ground that can lead to a resolution.

At this juncture, the parties delve deeper into areas of disagreement that surfaced during the discussion stage. These disagreements could be over various elements such as facts, assumptions, goals, values, or procedures. Each disagreement is carefully examined, and the differing viewpoints are laid out for consideration. By explicitly identifying these areas of conflict, the parties can gain a clearer understanding of what stands in the way of an agreement.

Understanding each party's viewpoints on these disagreements is a critical aspect of the clarification stage. This involves more than just acknowledging the differing perspectives; it requires a genuine attempt to understand the reasoning behind these viewpoints. It's essential to note that each party's stance is influenced by their interests, experiences, and values. Therefore, gaining insight into these aspects can shed light on why a particular position is held, making it easier to negotiate effectively.

The clarification stage also involves exploring potential reconciliations for the identified disagreements. This is where creativity and flexibility become crucial. The parties must brainstorm possible solutions that could resolve their conflicts. It's important to remember that negotiation is not about winning or losing; it's about finding a solution that satisfies all parties. Therefore, the potential reconciliation should be such that it addresses the concerns of all parties and is perceived as fair by everyone involved.

In essence, the clarification stage is about dissecting the problem and understanding it from all angles. It's about creating a roadmap for the negotiation, highlighting the obstacles and plotting potential paths around them. This stage requires patience, open-mindedness, and strong communication skills, setting the course for a successful negotiation.

Negotiation

This is the most important part of the negotiation process because this stage will determine the conclusion that will be reached by both parties. This also determines the so-called win-win decision, one that will benefit both parties in all circumstances.

Negotiation, in this sense, involves the following processes:

- **Negotiation proper**

This is the part where both parties give their arguments on the facts of the case or situation. These arguments may be based solely on the facts, on a company policy, or on a law effective in the place where each resides. This is also the part where both parties give suggestions, tips, or advice on how to settle disputes for their betterment. Most of the time, this part is the most difficult to finish because of the demands or settlements made by one party which may not turn out to be beneficial to the other. As such, extensive research and argumentation must be employed so as not to bring both parties to hostility.

- **Agreement**

This is the part where both parties finally agree to the suggestions, advice, and course of action formulated and discussed during the negotiation.

- **Execution**

This is the part where both parties put everything in writing so that whenever a dispute may once again arise because of the same set of facts and issues, the document embodying everything that has been discussed will be the reference to the course of action to be made. Usually, it is suggested that both parties must have a copy of the document embodying these matters, as this document will serve as a contract that is binding to both parties.

Implementation

The implementation phase marks the culmination of the negotiation process. Once an agreement has been reached, it is time to put the agreed-upon course of action into practice. This stage is about transforming the theoretical solutions discussed during the negotiation into tangible actions that can resolve the issue at hand.

In this stage, all parties involved have a responsibility to adhere strictly to what has been agreed upon. Deviating from the agreement can jeopardize the trust built during the negotiation process and could lead to further conflicts. Therefore, each party must be committed to fulfilling their part of the deal, ensuring that the agreement is honored in both letter and spirit.

The various stages of negotiation provide a framework that guides the process. This framework, while not foolproof, offers a structure that helps a negotiator understand their role and purpose in the negotiation. It provides a roadmap for navigating the complex dynamics of negotiation, helping the negotiator serve not just their interests, but also those of the other party.

This framework, with stages ranging from preparation to implementation, is generally sufficient to guide a negotiator through most scenarios. However, it is important to remember that negotiation is a flexible process that may require adaptability and improvisation depending on the unique circumstances of each situation.

While we've delved into the mechanics of how negotiation works, it's crucial to remember that negotiation is not a one-size-fits-all solution. It is not always the answer to every problem. There are situations where negotiation may not be possible or beneficial, such as when one party refuses to engage in good faith or when there is a significant imbalance of power.

However, there are many situations where negotiation is not just helpful, but crucial. In conflicts where there is a need for a mutually agreeable solution, or where maintaining relationships is important, negotiation becomes an indispensable tool. By enabling parties to work together to find a resolution that serves everyone's interests, negotiation fosters collaboration, understanding, and ultimately, resolution.

Chapter 3: Situations Where Negotiation is Crucial

Nobody wants to go to court and pursue a case against another because of the relatively high cost of litigation. Neither does anyone want to go to court and defend their cause because failing to do so may damage one's reputation.

As such, even the law requires that as much as possible, parties must resort first to negotiation or amicable settlement so as to avoid prolonging the issues brought about by court processes. While it is true that litigation will end controversies, it is still highly recommended that parties settle their issues first among themselves.

Negotiation is crucial in the following situations:

Settlement of Debt

Negotiation is crucial in this situation because it will eventually evolve into a collection case if no conversation ensues between both parties. Since most of the time, debts are governed by contracts; the breach of the latter may subject the offending party to legal repercussions.

Whenever a debt is incurred by one party, the other party may demand payment depending on the agreed terms and conditions. If after the due date, the debtor does not pay, the creditor will send a demand letter with the assistance of a lawyer, such that if the debtor does not heed to his demands, the creditor will file a case against him.

Negotiation is crucial in this case because even before a lawsuit is commenced, the parties are given an opportunity to settle the issue amongst their selves. It lessens the liability that one party will answer, and it will make things easier for the other to pursue his interests. For instance, the debtor may ask for an extension of the due date for additional interest, or he may ask to pay on another date with an increased amount.

Employment Termination Because of Authorized Cases

Negotiation is also crucial whenever employment termination due to authorized causes happens. Termination due to authorized cause is a situation in which the employment contract of employees is stopped or terminated because of causes within the control of the employee. Simply put, employees are removed from their jobs because the employer is authorized to do so under the law.

Some of the authorized causes are the following:

- **Installation of labor-saving devices**

Companies install labor-saving devices as a way to reduce costs and increase efficiency in the method of production. This involves replacing manual labor with automated labor by installing machines and robotic equipment. In this situation, the employer installs these devices while at the same time terminating the employment of those who are replaced by these machines.

- **Redundancy**

Redundancy happens when an employer has employees in excess of what is reasonably required by the enterprise. There is redundancy when a position is superfluous. It usually happens when the employer over-hires workers, when the establishment decreases its capacity, when two or more companies merge or consolidate, and when the business drops one of its product lines or services. In these cases, because a position is occupied by two or more people, the employer needs to retain one and remove the others by terminating their employment contract.

- **Retrenchment to prevent losses**

Retrenchment is the reduction of employees to cut down costs of operations, particularly salaries and wages of employees, mainly because a business suffers losses in its operations. Simply put, the employer removes employees because the business suffers losses due to operations and because retaining them will mean more losses.

- **Business closure**

An employer is also allowed to remove employees from work due to the closure of business. Of course, it must be noted that the removal of employees due to closure must not be associated with intent to avoid liabilities.

In any of these cases, negotiation is crucial because the employees' compensation and rights are both affected. If these rights are violated, employees will have a cause of action against the employer, and if not negotiated, they will have no choice but to file an employment dispute with government agencies. Negotiation serves to clarify to the employees the reasons why their employment is terminated, the legal basis of such removal, and the benefits that they are entitled to because of these causes.

Contract Signing

Negotiation plays a pivotal role in the formation and execution of contracts. It is the mechanism through which the parties involved express their intentions, expectations, and requirements, shaping the terms and conditions of the contract. Without negotiation, the true intent of the parties entering into the contract might not be fully understood or adequately addressed.

Contracts are more than just legal documents; they represent agreements between two or more parties that outline specific obligations and expectations. These obligations could involve performing a certain task, providing a service, or refraining from doing something. Once agreed upon, these contracts become binding laws between the parties involved, governing their relationship and interactions regarding the matter at hand.

For instance, consider a scenario where one party wishes to sell a piece of land to another. In this case, both the seller and the buyer enter the negotiation with their respective interests. The buyer, for example, may want the land to be delivered clean, and devoid of any buildings or improvements. On the other hand, the seller's interest might lie in receiving payment in cash.

Negotiation ensures that these individual intentions are effectively communicated, understood, and incorporated into the contract. It provides a platform where the buyer and seller can discuss their expectations, negotiate terms that satisfy both parties and create an agreement that reflects these mutual understandings.

Moreover, negotiation helps in resolving any discrepancies or conflicts that may arise during the drafting of the contract. Through dialogue and compromise, the parties can find solutions that honor their respective needs and wants.

In essence, negotiation breathes life into the contract, transforming it from a mere document into a dynamic agreement that encapsulates the intentions and expectations of all parties involved. It ensures that the contract truly serves its purpose - to facilitate a fair and mutually beneficial arrangement between the parties.

Insurance Policies

Negotiating is a fundamental aspect of many business transactions, and obtaining insurance policies is no exception. Typically, insurance policies are presented as adhesive contracts, which are essentially 'take it or leave it' agreements. The insurer provides the potential client with predefined terms and conditions, leaving the client with the decision to either accept or reject them.

However, this doesn't mean that there's no room for negotiation. In fact, negotiation plays a critical role in ensuring that the policies are fully understood by the client and that there are no provisions that could be disadvantageous to one or both parties involved.

Understanding an insurance policy can be quite challenging due to the complex language and terms used. Through negotiation, the client can seek clarification on any confusing terms or conditions, ensuring that they fully comprehend what they're signing up for. This not only helps the client make an informed decision but also protects them from potential disputes or misunderstandings down the line.

Moreover, negotiation allows the client to voice their concerns and needs. They may find certain terms unacceptable or feel that some important aspects aren't adequately covered. In such cases, negotiating with the insurance provider could lead to modifications that make the policy more aligned with the client's needs.

On the other hand, insurance providers also benefit from these negotiations. It gives them a chance to explain their policies better and reassure the client about the benefits and protections they're offering. Additionally, it allows them to understand the client's needs better, which can help them tailor their products and services more effectively.

Negotiation also opens up the possibility of finding a middle ground. Some terms might not be ideal for either party, and negotiation can help tweak these terms to ensure mutual benefit. This can lead to a more balanced, fair policy that serves both parties' best interests.

While insurance policies often come as adhesive contracts, negotiation remains a crucial part of the process. It helps ensure clear understanding, mutual satisfaction, and fair provisions, ultimately leading to a beneficial agreement for both the client and the insurer. Therefore, clients are encouraged to not shy away from negotiating their insurance policies. After all, negotiation is not just about getting the best deal; it's also about ensuring clarity, fairness, and peace of mind.

Family Matters

Negotiation isn't just for boardrooms and legal contracts; it's equally relevant and critical in the realm of family matters. From seemingly small decisions like choosing a movie for a family Sunday movie night to more significant issues like selling the family car to raise funds, negotiation plays a pivotal role in resolving disputes and reaching consensus within the family.

The importance of negotiation in family matters stems from the fact that any decision taken within this context can have far-reaching effects. It's not just about the immediate outcomes or the material well-being of the family. The decisions made can profoundly impact the relationships between family members, shaping the dynamics within the family unit.

For instance, if one family member unilaterally decides to sell the family car without consulting others, it could lead to feelings of resentment and exclusion. On the other hand, a negotiation process where everyone's views are heard and considered can lead to a solution that everyone agrees with, thereby promoting harmony and mutual respect.

Interestingly, many families engage in negotiation processes without even realizing it. Deciding on weekend activities, planning holiday trips, or setting household rules - all these involve elements of negotiation. When family members express their preferences, listen to each other, and work together to find a solution that satisfies everyone, they are, in essence, negotiating.

Understanding this can help families manage conflicts better and make more inclusive decisions. By consciously adopting negotiation techniques, families can ensure that every member feels heard and valued. This not only promotes better decision-making but also strengthens the bonds between family members.

Negotiation is a powerful tool in the context of family matters. When used effectively, it can aid in making fair decisions, resolving conflicts, and fostering a sense of unity and mutual respect among family members.

Business decisions

Negotiation is crucial in business decisions because one act may or may not be beneficial to its well-being. Unless supplied by the entrepreneur's own funds, a business affects not only its owners but also its stakeholders and investors who have placed large sums of money on it. As such, whenever the business engages in a transaction, especially for large purchases, negotiation is essential not only between the parties but also among the owners of the business.

It can be said that negotiation is very important in making business decisions because one wrong decision can cause the downfall of the whole business. While it is true that business losses are usually associated with faulty operations, it is also true that these losses are caused by faulty decision-making. As such, it is highly encouraged that in cases of disputes, whether internal or external in nature, negotiators must also have a background of what the business is and how things work.

Prenuptial agreement

Negotiation is also crucial in prenuptial agreements. Most jurisdictions have different rules and regulations pertaining to weddings. Some require the commencement of a prenuptial agreement so that after marriage, both the families of the groom and the bride will know how their relationship will be governed. For instance, they might agree that donations given to either the groom or the bride will belong to them jointly. Negotiation makes sure that these provisions and desires are made known so as to establish a good working relationship.

Criminal Engagement

Negotiation is crucial in criminal engagement, especially in cases where there are hostages. Negotiation serves as the bridge to create tranquility between law enforcement officers and the offenders, so as to prevent more harm.

Negotiation, in general, is essential in these situations to be able to maintain a good working relationship, to clarify reasons and bases for certain actions, to bring about a new set of terms and conditions between the parties, and to arrive at a settlement instead of proceeding to litigation.

Chapter 4: Steps to Master the Art of Negotiation

Negotiation is a skill that must be mastered to be rendered effectively. While some may think that it is hard to negotiate, it is a fact that it can be mastered by practice and regular engagement.

To be able to master the art of negotiation, one must do the following:

1. Practice problem analysis

Analyzing problems is undoubtedly the cornerstone of successful negotiation. As you delve into the complexities of negotiation, you'll quickly realize that every disagreement, suggestion, argument, and potential plan of action hinges on the problem at hand. By thoroughly analyzing the issue, you not only uncover the root cause but also identify the parties affected and interested, as well as the objectives that need to be achieved.

However, problem analysis isn't as straightforward as simply identifying cause and effect. It requires a deeper level of understanding. You must first determine the facts, and then understand the elements surrounding the problem. This involves an exploration of the potential causes that may have led to the current situation. The aim here is to gain a comprehensive understanding of the problem's origin in order to devise the most effective solution.

Furthermore, problem analysis requires anticipation of the possible consequences of every course of action. This step necessitates strategic thinking and foresight. You need to think about how each action will ripple out into the future and what impacts it might have. By doing so, you can avoid unintended negative outcomes and ensure your actions align with your goals.

Finally, problem analysis involves outlining the potential courses of action that could lead to achieving the desired goal. This requires creativity and flexibility, as you explore all available options and compare their merits and drawbacks. In essence, problem analysis is about leaving no stone unturned and doing everything within your power to reach your ultimate objective.

So, as you navigate through negotiations, remember that problem analysis isn't just a task to be completed - it's a process of discovery. It's about uncovering the facts, predicting the future, and charting the best course forward. It's about being thorough, thoughtful, and proactive to ensure you reach your goal.

2. Prepare for the meeting

Just as students arm themselves with knowledge before stepping into a classroom, so too must negotiators come to the table fully prepared. Imagine yourself in the role of a negotiator. You must be thoroughly acquainted with the issue at hand, just like a student must understand their coursework. This involves not only grasping the basic facts but also comprehending the underlying complexities and nuances.

Next, consider your objectives. What are the goals you are striving to achieve on behalf of the party you represent? Have these clearly defined in your mind, much like a student would have specific learning outcomes they're working towards. Understanding these goals will guide your strategy and help you stay focused during the negotiation process.

Now, think about your plan of action. What options and alternatives do you have if your primary plan doesn't pan out? Just as a student might have a study plan B in case their initial approach doesn't yield the desired results, you too must be agile and adaptable, ready to switch gears if necessary.

Consider also the areas where you can make trade-offs. These are like the points on which a student might need to compromise to balance their academic workload. Recognizing what you're willing to give in exchange for what you want is a crucial part of successful negotiation.

Finally, take a step back and consider the broader context. Understand the history of the relationship between the parties involved, akin to a student understanding the historical context of their subject matter. Have there been past negotiations between these parties? What were the outcomes? Identifying common goals and areas of agreement from past interactions can provide valuable insights for your current negotiation.

In essence, preparing for a negotiation is akin to preparing for an important exam. You need to know your material, understand your objectives, have a plan (and a backup plan), be ready for compromise, and understand the historical context. So, as you step into your next negotiation, remember to prepare thoroughly. Your success depends on it.

3. Actively listen

As a negotiator, mastering the art of active listening is absolutely crucial. Imagine yourself in a negotiation. You can't effectively counter an argument or propose viable solutions without first fully understanding the other party's perspective and goals. It's like trying to answer a question without knowing what's being asked.

Active listening involves more than just hearing the words that are spoken. It requires you to engage deeply with the speaker, to really tune into their message. This includes picking up on their verbal cues – the tone, inflection, and emphasis they use. But it also involves reading their non-verbal language – their body language, facial expressions, and gestures. These subtle cues can often reveal more about the speaker's true feelings and intentions than their words alone.

Consider the benefits of truly listening. When you actively listen, you're more likely to find areas where compromise is possible. This is similar to finding common ground in a debate. By understanding the other party's needs and wants, you can identify potential areas of agreement or trade-offs that could bring both parties closer to a resolution.

However, remember that negotiation isn't a monologue. Simply stating your arguments and ignoring the other party's input won't lead to a successful outcome. After all, the ultimate goal of negotiation isn't to win an argument but to reach a mutually beneficial settlement.

To achieve this, you must genuinely listen to the other party. Understand their viewpoint, consider their proposals, and respond thoughtfully. This approach not only helps to build trust and rapport, but also increases the likelihood of reaching a resolution that both parties are happy with. So, as you step into your next negotiation, remember to listen actively. Your success may depend on it.

4. Control Emotions

As a negotiator, maintaining control over your emotions is paramount. Imagine yourself in a negotiation scenario. The conversation should be objective, with arguments grounded in facts, information, laws, policies, and clear reasoning. Emotions have no place in this dialogue, as they could potentially sabotage rather than foster relationships between the parties.

Think of negotiation as a game of chess. Each move should be calculated and strategic, not dictated by emotional impulses. Letting frustration, anger, or impatience seep into your negotiation can skew your judgment and lead to decisions that aren't in your best interest or that of the party you represent.

It's natural to feel frustrated when negotiations become challenging. Perhaps one party is doggedly pursuing a particular course of action that you don't agree with. However, allowing these emotions to dictate your actions can lead to unfavorable outcomes. For instance, if frustration gets the better of you, you might be tempted to hastily agree to the other party's proposal just to end the negotiation.

While this may bring about a temporary resolution, it doesn't address the true intent of the negotiation. The agreement reached under such circumstances may not reflect the genuine needs and wants of both parties. It's like winning a battle but losing the war – you've resolved the immediate conflict but potentially jeopardized future negotiations and relationships.

Therefore, it's essential to keep your emotions in check during negotiations. Stay calm, composed, and focused on the goal at hand. Remember that negotiation is a process, not a one-time event. It requires patience, perseverance, and a level-headed approach. By controlling your emotions, you increase your chances of reaching an agreement that truly reflects the interests of all parties involved.

5. Communicate Verbally and In Person

As a negotiator, effective communication is a skill you must master. Picture yourself in the midst of a negotiation. Your ability to articulate your party's interests, sentiments, and goals clearly could mean the difference between success and failure. Miscommunication or misunderstanding can lead to conflict or failed negotiations, so sharpening your verbal communication skills is crucial.

Think of your words as tools. You must use them skillfully to convey your message, ensuring that your points are understood as intended. This involves more than just speaking eloquently. It means choosing the right words, structuring your thoughts logically, and delivering your message in a way that resonates with the other party.

While non-verbal communication can supplement your words, it should never replace verbal communication. Non-verbal cues like body language, facial expressions, and gestures can be open to interpretation and may unintentionally send mixed signals. Therefore, always prioritize verbal communication to ensure your message is clear and unambiguous.

Moreover, whenever possible, strive to communicate in person. In our digital age, it might be tempting to rely on teleconferencing or videoconferencing for negotiations. However, there's no substitute for face-to-face interaction. When you're physically present in a meeting, you're able to read the room better, pick up on subtle cues, and establish a stronger rapport with the other party.

Being physically present in a negotiation also conveys your commitment to reaching a resolution. It shows that you're willing to invest your time and effort into the process, which can encourage the other party to do the same. So, as you step into your next negotiation, remember the importance of clear, verbal communication and, if possible, insist on doing it in person. Your success may depend on it.

6. Work With a Team

As a negotiator, you might be the one leading the discussions, but remember that negotiation is not a solo act. It's akin to a team sport where each player has a crucial role. Behind every successful negotiation, there's often a team working tirelessly in the background, researching, strategizing, and supporting the negotiator.

Think of yourself as the captain of a ship. You steer the vessel, but you rely on your crew to navigate, maintain the ship, and look out for potential obstacles. Similarly, in a negotiation, you need a support system. This team can help you prepare for the negotiation, providing valuable insights, information, and perspectives that you might not have considered.

Your team can consist of individuals from various departments or areas within your organization. Each member brings unique expertise and viewpoints to the table, fostering a comprehensive approach to negotiation. For instance, a financial expert can provide insights into budgetary constraints, a legal advisor can ensure compliance with laws and regulations, and a marketing specialist can offer a customer-centric perspective.

Involving your team in the negotiation process also promotes a sense of ownership and collaboration. When everyone feels they are part of the process, they are more likely to support the final decision. Remember, the purpose of negotiation isn't just about winning an argument or getting the best deal. It's about resolving disputes and controversies in a way that satisfies all parties involved.

So, as you step into your next negotiation, remember to involve your team. Seek their input, value their contributions, and work together towards a common goal. The collective wisdom of a team often leads to better outcomes than what one individual can achieve alone.

7. Practice Problem-Solving

Problem analysis will be of no meaning if it cannot be solved. As such, negotiators must also master their problem-solving skills because providing courses of action or plans is the expected output of negotiation.

In this sense, the negotiator must learn to incorporate the following matters in problem-solving:

- **Goals:** The negotiator must keep in mind the goals of his party. While he must pursue the interests of his party, he must, nevertheless, obtain the goals of the other party to reach a win-win situation.
- **Trades**: Along with their respective goals, the negotiators must be able to determine what both parties are willing to trade (or to give up) to attain their goals.
- **Alternatives**: If the parties do not agree on the initial plan of settlement, the negotiators must be able to provide alternatives. They must be able to convey to

the other party the importance of settling the case, and they must be able to inform the other party of the possible consequences on their part should they not agree to settle it immediately.

- **Relationships**: Negotiators must also have a brief history of past relationships between the parties. At times, difficulty in reaching an amicable settlement is experienced not because one party is not willing to settle the issue, but because of a bad experience that one party has experienced in dealing with another. As such, negotiators must also learn to take advantage of the relationships, for this can reveal the success or failure of the negotiation.
- **Consequences**: Negotiators must have an idea of the possible consequences of the actions decided upon. Although one action has been agreed upon, the negotiators must be able to convey to their respective parties the effects of doing such action not only to their own parties but also to the others involved. Negotiators must also be able to convey to both parties the consequences of the actions or solutions to third persons, or to those who do not have any interest in the transaction or case.
- **Influence**: Negotiators must also determine who among the two parties has the greatest influence or power. They must be able to determine who will lose or gain more when an action is implemented.

A negotiator who solves a problem while taking into consideration these factors will surely be able to see the bigger picture of the issue.

8. Practice Decision-Making

As a negotiator, your ability to make swift, informed decisions is crucial. Imagine yourself in the heat of a negotiation. The room is buzzing with differing opinions, offers, and counter-offers. In this dynamic environment, indecisiveness could lead to a deadlock or, worse, give the opposing party an upper hand.

You're not just a participant in these negotiations; you're a decision-maker. You're there to advocate for your party's interests, and to do so effectively, you must be able to make quick, yet thoughtful decisions. It's like being a chess player, anticipating the other player's moves and responding swiftly and strategically.

The importance of decision-making in negotiation cannot be overstated. Decisive action often paves the way for offers and counter-offers, pushing the negotiation forward. As long as there is disagreement among parties, these offers and counter-offers will keep surfacing. Therefore, you must be prepared to make decisions not only on the main issue at hand but also on these ensuing offers and counter-offers.

However, decision-making isn't just about speed; it's also about precision. You must balance the need to act quickly with the requirement to make informed decisions. This involves thorough preparation before the negotiation, including understanding your party's interests, researching the other party's likely positions, and considering possible outcomes.

So, as you walk into your next negotiation, remember the importance of decisive action. Practice your decision-making skills, anticipate various scenarios, and be prepared to make informed decisions on the spot. Remember, every decision you make can significantly impact the negotiation's outcome, so make each one count.

9. Master Interpersonal Skills

As a negotiator, mastering interpersonal skills is as important as understanding the intricacies of the deal. Picture yourself in the midst of a negotiation. You're not just dealing with facts, figures, and legal terms; you're dealing with people. Your ability to build strong relationships, not only with your own party but also with the other party, can significantly influence the negotiation's outcome.

Imagine your negotiation as a dance. It requires patience, understanding, and the ability to move in sync with your partner. The same applies to negotiation. Patience allows you to stay calm and composed, even when discussions become heated or complex. It enables you to listen actively, understand the other party's perspective, and respond thoughtfully.

Persuasion is another essential interpersonal skill for a negotiator. However, it's important to remember that persuasion is not about manipulating others or forcing your views onto them. Instead, it's about presenting your arguments convincingly, appealing to their interests, and demonstrating how your proposal can benefit them.

Maintaining a positive atmosphere during negotiations, especially difficult ones, is crucial. This involves showing respect for all parties involved, managing conflicts constructively, and fostering open communication. A positive atmosphere can enhance cooperation, promote mutual understanding, and increase the likelihood of reaching a satisfactory agreement.

So, as you step into your next negotiation, remember the importance of interpersonal skills. Cultivate patience, practice your persuasion techniques, and strive to create a positive environment. These skills, combined with your negotiation strategies, can help you navigate the complexities of negotiation and achieve successful outcomes.

10. Observe Ethical Standards

As a negotiator, you must always prioritize displaying commendable behavior in the presence of the other party. This includes refraining from using language that is vulgar, explicit, or inappropriate when expressing your concerns or points of view. Communication is key in negotiations, and the manner in which you communicate can greatly impact the outcome.

Moreover, it's essential to avoid resorting to physical or emotional violence, even when disagreements arise or your demands aren't met. It's natural for negotiations to have moments of tension, but it's crucial to handle these situations with grace and patience. Remember, the goal is to reach a mutually beneficial agreement, not to win an argument.

Furthermore, maintaining ethical conduct should be your standard, even if the negotiation seems unproductive or headed toward a stalemate. The way you conduct yourself during these challenging times truly defines your character as a negotiator. It's not about forcing your way to an agreement, but about fostering understanding and finding common ground.

Developing these skills and following these steps are central to mastering the art of negotiation. With practice and perseverance, it's possible for you to effectively apply these techniques in critical situations. Remember, negotiation isn't just about closing a deal; it's a valuable skill that can help resolve conflicts and build relationships in various aspects of life. By honing these skills, you're not only becoming a better negotiator but also enhancing your ability to navigate complex interpersonal dynamics.

Chapter 5: Get What You Deserve

Negotiation does not ensure victory for only one party. Its goal is for both parties to benefit from the agreed course of action. This is what everyone deserves to get.

Nevertheless, it is a must that the negotiator knows not only how to give advice, but also what he will get by performing the same. The following are some of the benefits that a negotiator gets:

Established Reputation

If a negotiator is an independent one, companies will not be afraid to seek his assistance in future disputes. A negotiator with an established reputation suggests that he has wide experience in handling settlement disputes and that he has mastered the art of negotiation. As such, his services will mean the success or failure of a cause or an establishment.

Employment

Negotiators can also have employment opportunities, especially for those who are always met with legal disputes. Instead of hiring a lawyer and filing a case in court, negotiators can be sought, and their services can be availed of not just by one party, but also by both parties. This method saves a lot of money that would have to be spent on litigation.

If the negotiators are already employed by companies, they have an opportunity to be transferred to the legal department or to a higher position. Because of their skills, they might even be transferred to management positions.

Fees

There are some companies that give fees to negotiators as payment for their services. As such, negotiators can earn money by assisting their clients in any dispute that they might meet.

There are some negotiators who render their services for free. Nevertheless, companies still give them compensation as payment for their services not only in settling the present dispute but also in saving them from possible litigation and tarnished reputation.

Established reliability

Because of their ability to settle disputes without resorting to litigation, negotiators can enhance their legitimacy in different situations, such as trade associations, political pressures, and management. The more a negotiator knows about the adverse party's objectives, the more powerful he is during negotiation, even though its subject is different from what he is accustomed to settling.

Knowledge

Negotiators will also have vast knowledge of the business of both parties, which can be used in future settlement disputes involving businesses that have the same nature. Also, knowledge of the products or the business itself, the market where it operates, the regulations governing it, and the legal requirements and formalities can be a source of power and reliability that the negotiator can tap into in future settlements.

Established courage

Negotiators who are willing to accept greater risks are usually seen to be better negotiators than those who are not. Similar to the basic concept of risk, the higher the presence of risk, the higher the return will be. The more the negotiator is familiar with different scenarios of settlement disputes, the more he will be able to understand what the other party wants and needs. This can also increase his power in determining solutions that are beneficial for both parties.

Negotiation skills not only bring success in a dispute but also provide benefits for the negotiators themselves. Through careful observation and practice, one can master the art of negotiation and use it to their advantage in various situations. Remember, getting what you deserve is not just about winning a dispute, but also ensuring that both parties benefit from the agreed course of action. By following these steps and honing your skills, you can become a successful negotiator who can create win-win situations for everyone involved. So go ahead and start practicing, and watch as your negotiation skills become a valuable asset in both your personal and professional life. Happy negotiating!

Chapter 6: Common Negotiation Pitfalls and How to Avoid Them

Negotiation is a delicate art, and even the most experienced negotiators can sometimes fall into certain traps. Here are some of the most common negotiation pitfalls and strategies on how to avoid them:

1. Being overly aggressive or overly submissive

- **Pitfall**: One common mistake is going to one of two extremes: being too aggressive and trying to dominate the negotiation, or being too submissive and giving in too easily.
- **Avoidance Strategy**: Strive for balance. Be assertive but respectful, making sure to firmly express your needs while also considering the needs of the other party.

2. Failing to listen

- **Pitfall**: Many negotiators focus so much on getting their own points across that they fail to listen to the other party.
- **Avoidance Strategy**: Active listening is key in negotiations. Ensure you understand the other party's perspective and needs by asking clarifying questions and summarizing what they've said to confirm your understanding.

3. Not preparing adequately

- **Pitfall**: Entering a negotiation without adequate preparation can lead to poor outcomes.
- **Avoidance Strategy**: Prior to the negotiation, research the other party, understand the market situation, set clear objectives, anticipate counterarguments, and prepare responses.

4. Letting emotions control the negotiation

- **Pitfall**: It's easy to let emotions take over, especially if the negotiation becomes heated. This can lead to irrational decisions or damage to the relationship with the other party.
- **Avoidance Strategy**: Practice emotional intelligence. Stay calm, maintain your composure, and don't take things personally. Remember, it's about the problem, not the person.

5. Not Having a Clear BATNA (Best Alternative To a Negotiated Agreement)

- **Pitfall**: If you don't have a clear idea of what your alternatives are, you might agree to a deal that is worse than what you could have achieved otherwise.
- **Avoidance Strategy**: Before entering the negotiation, know your BATNA. This will give you a clear idea of when to walk away and when to push for more.

By being aware of these common pitfalls and developing strategies to avoid them, you can significantly improve your negotiation skills and outcomes.

Conclusion

Congratulations! You've reached the end of this comprehensive journey into the art of negotiation. It's no small feat, and you should be proud of the commitment you've shown to personal growth and development.

Throughout this guide, you've learned that successful negotiation isn't about domination, but about a dance of diplomacy, a harmonious exchange of interests. You've understood that it's not merely about winning, but about seeking a balance between your aspirations and those of the other party.

Remember, mastering negotiation is a skill that requires consistent practice, patience, and resilience. It's about articulating your needs effectively while being receptive to the needs of others. You've now grasped the concept that preparation is crucial and that leveraging the principles of persuasion can tilt negotiations in your favor.

One of the key insights from this guide is the importance of emotional intelligence in negotiation. By regulating your emotions and empathizing with the other party, you can foster stronger connections and achieve more favorable outcomes. And let's not forget, that negotiation isn't just about the present moment. It's about cultivating relationships that will yield benefits in the long run.

Now comes the exciting part - applying these insights. I strongly encourage you to put these newfound skills into action. Start with low-stakes negotiations, maybe with friends or family members. As you gain confidence, you can then apply these techniques in more complex situations. Remember, every negotiation, whether big or small, is an opportunity for learning and growth.

Bear in mind, that even the most skilled negotiators don't always secure what they initially set out for. There will be times when you'll have to compromise or even walk away. That's perfectly fine. The crux of negotiation lies in approaching each situation with an open mind, a readiness to understand the other party, and a commitment to finding a mutually beneficial resolution.

The journey of negotiation mastery is continuous. As you grow more adept, there will always be more to discover, more strategies to learn, and more nuances to understand. But with each negotiation, you'll become better, more self-assured, and more effective.

You've taken a significant step in your journey by completing this guide. Now, it's time to stride forward. Venture out and negotiate. Exercise your new skills. Reflect on your experiences. And remember, every negotiation, irrespective of the outcome, is progress in your journey to mastering the art of negotiation.

So here's to you, for finishing this guide and for embarking on this transformative journey. Keep going, keep learning, and keep negotiating. You're well on your way to becoming a master negotiator. Congratulations once again!

FAQs

What is negotiation?

Negotiation is a procedure in which two or more groups with diverse interests engage in dialogue to arrive at a mutually agreeable resolution. It necessitates communication, convincing arguments, and compromise, making it an essential skill in both personal and professional realms.

Why is mastering negotiation important?

Mastering negotiation can lead to better outcomes in various aspects of life, from securing a higher salary or lower price for a product to resolving conflicts and building stronger relationships. It allows you to effectively express your needs and understand the needs of others, resulting in win-win situations.

How can I improve my negotiation skills?

Improving your negotiation skills involves a combination of learning and practice. You can learn about negotiation strategies, principles of persuasion, and emotional intelligence through books, courses, and guides. Practicing these skills in real-life scenarios, starting with low-stakes situations, can help you become more confident and effective.

What role does emotional intelligence play in negotiation?

Emotional intelligence plays a crucial role in negotiation. It helps you manage your emotions, understand the emotions of the other party, and respond effectively. Being emotionally intelligent can help you build rapport, empathize with others, and ultimately achieve better negotiation outcomes.

How should I prepare for a negotiation?

Preparation for a negotiation involves understanding your needs and those of the other party, defining your goals, and developing a strategy. Researching the issue at hand, knowing your best alternative to a negotiated agreement (BATNA), and practicing your communication skills can also be beneficial.

What should I do if a negotiation isn't going in my favor?

If a negotiation isn't going in your favor, it's important to stay calm and composed. Try to understand the other party's perspective and restate your needs clearly. If an agreement still seems unlikely, it might be best to take a break, reassess your strategy, or consider walking away.

Can anyone become a good negotiator?

Absolutely! While some people may naturally have traits that make them effective negotiators, negotiation is a skill that anyone can learn and improve with knowledge, practice, and patience. Remember, mastering negotiation is a journey, not a destination.

References and Helpful Links

Curtis, G. (2023, December 6). How to master the art of negotiation. Investopedia. https://www.investopedia.com/articles/pf/07/negotiation_tips.asp

Gibson, B. (2023, October 13). Negotiation strategies: Top strategies for negotiation | Vistage. Vistage Research Center. https://www.vistage.com/research-center/business-growth-strategy/six-successful-strategies-for-negotiation/

MindTools | Home. (n.d.). https://www.mindtools.com/a8vrkes/10-common-negotiation-mistakes

6 Negotiation skills all professionals can benefit from. (2023, May 11). Business Insights Blog. https://online.hbs.edu/blog/post/negotiation-skills

S, P. (2023, June 25). Importance of negotiation. https://www.linkedin.com/pulse/importance-negotiation-priyadharshini-s

Dhir, R. (2023, October 31). Negotiation: definition, stages, skills, and strategies. Investopedia. https://www.investopedia.com/terms/n/negotiation.asp

Super. (2023, October 22). Top 4 Reasons Why Negotiation Skills are Very Important in the Business World. Visit → strengthscape.com. https://strengthscape.com/top-4-reasons-why-negotiation-skills-are-very-important-in-the-business-world/

www.ingramcontent.com/pod-product-compliance
Lightning Source LLC
Chambersburg PA
CBHW030536220526
45463CB00007B/2855